FIND MOMO EVERYWHERE

WORDS AND PICTURES BY ANDREW KNAPP

NEW YORK TIMES BEST-SELLING CREATOR

QUIRK BOOKS

PHILADELPHIA

This is the story of Momo.
Have you had a friend this true?

The best around
with four paws on the ground,
who spends all of their time
with you.

We'd fetch and we'd catch,
we'd run and we'd jump.
Every day we found new
games to play.

But our favorite, you see, was hide-and-go-seek . . .
and Momo could play this all day.

From the porch
to the yard,
some spots were
quite hard!

Can you find him?
Where did he go?

He hid inside and out,
upstairs and down.

Once we found the
best spots, our game
had to grow.

We crossed valleys and mountains and fields of snow.
In our big yellow bus we had places to go!

Can you find a fish?

Can you find a deer?

Now let's find Momo!
Is he far? Is he near?

Let's go watch the
sunrise in Paris!

Can you find a bike?

Can you find a
red flower?

Now let's find Momo!
Is that him by the
Eiffel Tower?

Café Caché

Can you find a cat?

And a red hydrant, too?

Now let's find Momo
behind something blue!

There were moments between that were calm and serene.

We would watch and listen and breathe . . .

When the rivers got cold,
and the trees turned to gold

and the ground was
covered in leaves.

And much like the seasons, time changed Momo, too.
Sometimes life won't allow us to keep what we knew.

His eyes had grown wiser, his fur turned to gray.
Even his games became harder to play.

Momo was old
and his body grew weak,
so I carried my friend
down to the creek.

With his favorite stick,
on his coziest bed,
for the very last time
he rested his head.

Momo had died.

I missed him.

I cried.

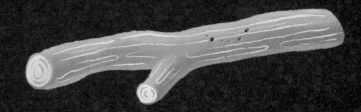

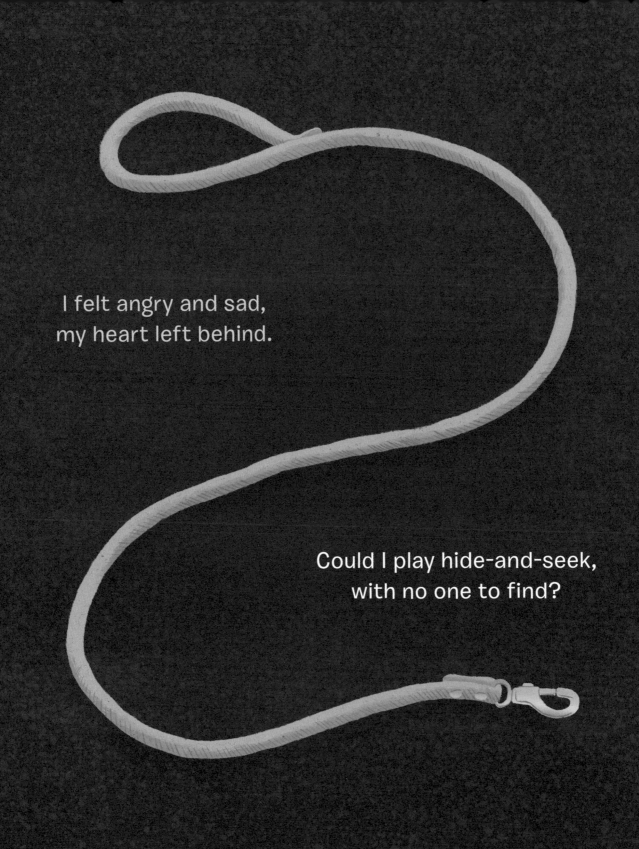

I felt angry and sad,
my heart left behind.

Could I play hide-and-seek,
with no one to find?

But if Momo was here,
I know what he'd say:

"It's okay to be sad,
but I want you to play!"

If I close my eyes, I can still reminisce—
the softness and smell of his fur that I miss.

And I'm sure that I'll find, when I look around,
That so long as I love him, he still can be found.

Found in a new morning sun shining bright.
Found in the moonlight and stars in the night.

As long as the mountains and rivers and birds
are singing their songs that Momo once heard . . .

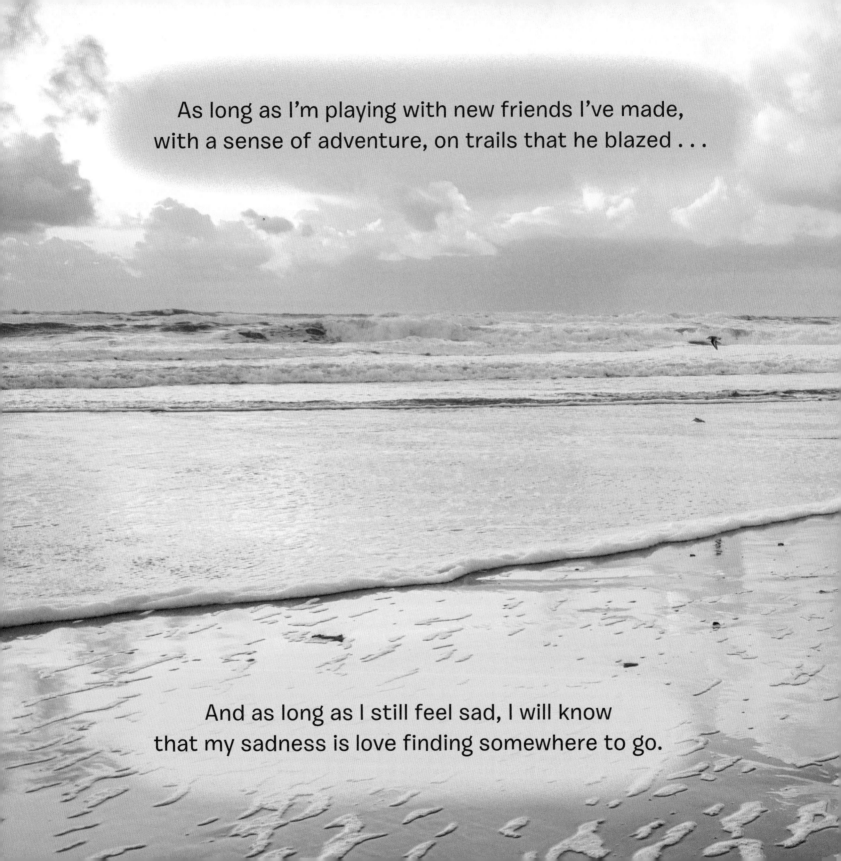

As long as I'm playing with new friends I've made,
with a sense of adventure, on trails that he blazed . . .

And as long as I still feel sad, I will know
that my sadness is love finding somewhere to go.

With new memories to make,
and new sights to share . . .

I know I can find
Momo everywhere.

For Momo, and for all the dogs we still find everywhere

A note about the art:
The mixed-media art in this book was created using a combination of Andrew Knapp's photography and illustration. Most of the photographs were taken with Momo nearby, and illustrations were integrated the way imperfectly recalled memories blend with the present.

Full Library of Congress Cataloging-in-Publication Data available upon request.

ISBN: 978-1-68369-386-4

Printed in China

Typeset in Burbank Small and Trend HM Sans

Designed by Paige Graff
Production management by John J. McGurk

Quirk Books
215 Church Street
Philadelphia, PA 19106
quirkbooks.com

10 9 8 7 6 5 4 3 2 1